The Little Book of Storytelling

Telling stories in the Early Years Foundation Stage

by Mary Medlicott
Illustrations by Martha Hardy

LITTLE **BOOKS WITH** **BIG** IDEAS

Published 2010 by A&C Black Publishers Limited
36 Soho Square, London W1D 3QY
www.acblack.com

ISBN 978-1-9041-8765-3

First published in the UK 2003 by Featherstone Education

Printed in Great Britain by Latimer Trend & Company Limited

This book is produced using paper that is made from wood grown in
managed, sustainable forests. It is natural, renewable and recyclable.

The logging and manufacturing processes conform to the environmental
regulations of the country of origin.

**To see our full range of titles
visit www.acblack.com**

Contents

Introduction – Telling, not reading   4–5

Section 1 – Storytelling

The benefits for children   6–7
The storyteller   8
Plus points for the storyteller   9
Engaging children's attention   10–11
Creating a good session   12–14

Section 2 – Using chants and rhymes

Twinkle, twinkle, little star   15–16
A forest adventure   17–18
The poor king and his goldfish   19–20
Davey Jones' sailors   21–23

Section 3 – Action stories

Going for a story walk   24–25
The far-away story walk   26
Wiggle-woof and waggle-woof   27–30
Flossie the flea takes a trip   31–32

Section 4 - Make a story

Using an object   33–34
Using a familiar theme   35–36
Using a puppet or toy   37–38
Using an actual event   39–40

Section 5 – True stories

A tale of your own   41–42
Involving the children   43–45

Section 6 – Other ways

Musical stories   46–47
Sound and movement   48–49

Section 7 – Traditional tales

The gingerbread man   50–53
The cat sat on the mat   54–56
The three wishes   57–58
The hat seller and the monkeys   59–62
Pinoncita   63–66

Section 8 – Hints for the storyteller

Remembering your story   67–68
Managing storytime   69–70
The wider context   71–72

Stories, Books and Resources   73–75

Introduction

Telling not reading

Storytelling, according to one old saying, is 'a habit older than writing and as common as bread.'

Long before books came into being, people realised that stories provide an ideal way of drawing young children into being interested and involved in the world about them.

Storytelling needs storytellers. This book provides all kinds of ideas and material for developing your skills and practice in this natural art – rhymes and chants that can lead into stories, action stories which make it easy for children to participate, plans for making up new stories, hints on telling your own true stories, and a good selection of folktales and other tales for passing on. Besides, there are hints on equally vital aspects such as preparing, remembering and presenting your stories and managing your storytelling sessions.

The book concentrates on storytelling 'out of your mouth' – in other words, storytelling without the book.

Compared with reading aloud, this provides a different and very refreshing way of telling stories and running storytimes. Freeing the storyteller to concentrate on the children, it enables the children, too, to concentrate in different and refreshing ways – giving their ideas, joining in rhymes and rhythms and generally feeling as though they are in the midst of the story. At the same time, storytelling without a book can greatly strengthen and support the use of books with children.

Not only does storytelling extend the children's interest in the many different kinds of stories, it encourages age-old techniques of communication which can be adapted for using with books – techniques such as using actions and facial expressions. Storytelling without a book can greatly boost the storyteller's confidence in being themselves, using their own natural ways of communicating in order to tell the story.

No matter where or when, storytelling has always been one of the central forms of education and entertainment among human beings. This book aims to encourage everyone who works (or lives) with young children to develop their interest and confidence in this fascinating activity.

The Benefits for Children

What do the children gain?

Storytelling gives children a reason to listen and something to remember. There are many benefits.

▶ **social** – storytelling teaches them to be part of a group

Coming together for a storytelling session gives young children valuable experience of listening and responding alongside others. Older or more confident children can encourage others by their example, teaching children not to be shy of joining in – and, equally important, how not to dominate by joining in too much!

▶ **linguistic** – storytelling gives them a rich experience of language

The rich wording and patterns of traditional stories give children experiences of language that are very different from the instructional and 'teaching' type of language they hear most often in class. Rhymes and other intriguing little patterns of words are literally 'ear-catching'. They encourage children to speak, repeating and echoing what they have heard.

▶ **imaginative** – storytelling encourages their own ideas

As a live experience, storytelling encourages children (and adults) to form their own pictures of what is going on. There are no 'correct' or 'incorrect' answers – children develop their own ideas of the story and can be encouraged to express these. The experience gives children real practice in thinking.

► **emotional** – storytelling helps them recognise feelings

The emotions of the characters and the listeners are central in storytelling. How a story feels is part and parcel of what happens. From experiencing the journey of the story, children can learn not only to recognise common emotions. They can also come to know that other people experience these too. Happiness, sadness, fear, anger – all are part of the repertoire of oral storytelling.

► **educational** – storytelling teaches them about the world

A rich variety of folktales can take children into the past and all the way round the world. This imaginative experience has wide educational value, especially for children whose own experiences of the world are limited. Introducing them to things they may never actually encounter in person, it helps children make sense of the world around them.

Storytelling also helps children to reach many of the Early Learning Goals:

Personal, social and emotional development (PSRN)

- continue to be interested, excited and motivated to learn
- be confident to try new activities, initiate ideas and speak in a group
- maintain attention, concentration and sit quietly when appropriate
- respond to experiences, showing a range of feelings when appropriate
- work as part of a group or class, taking turns and sharing fairly

Communication, language and literacy (CLL)

- interact with others, negotiating plans and taking turns in conversations
- enjoy listening to and using spoken language
- sustain attentive listening, responding to what they have heard by relevant comments, questions or actions
- listen with enjoyment and respond to stories, songs, rhymes and poems and make up their own stories, rhymes and poems
- extend their vocabulary, exploring the meanings and sounds of new words
- speak clearly and audibly with confidence and control
- use language to imagine and recreate roles and experiences
- use talk to organise, sequence and clarify thinking, ideas, feelings and events
- retell narratives in sequence drawing on the language patterns of stories
- show an understanding of elements of stories

Creative development (CD)

- use their imagination in role-play and stories
- express and communicate their ideas, thoughts and feelings

The Storyteller

'Can I do it?'

Many people find that once they start storytelling without a book, they discover a new feeling of confidence in themselves as the storyteller. Yet the prospect of putting aside the book can be a worrying experience. Here are some of the most common fears:

▶ **I haven't got a story to tell!**

But you probably know quite a few already. What about 'Going On A Bear Hunt?' Or 'Goldilocks and The Three Bears?' And how about telling a story from your own experience – a funny incident, or something a little bit spooky? Or could you try making up a story as you go along, perhaps with some help from your audience?

▶ **I'll never remember the story!**

You will if you prepare it first. There are many different ways of doing this (see pages 67-68) – and, for the telling itself, you could perhaps use story cards or props to help you. If you do forget, you could always ask the children what they think happens next and tell them you'll continue the story tomorrow!

▶ **The children won't listen without pictures to help them!**

The funny thing is that you may discover that they concentrate better. With actions, sounds and props to focus their attention, they may even enjoy and understand a told story better than a story from a book.

▶ **What if there's chaos and the children run riot?**

With rhymes and rhythms for joining in, there's far less likelihood of trouble and more chance of participation. If things do get a bit out of hand, however, you can always cut things short and try again another time.

Plus points for the storyteller

There are numerous advantages when you set aside the book and tell a story 'out of your mouth'. These range from the physical to the imaginative.

▶ Your arms are free

'Can't see the picture!' is a frequent cry when you're using a book. Your hands are trapped. Without the book your hands are free to make actions, form gestures to emphasise a point, or reach out to an unhappy child.

▶ Your eyes are free

Eyes are an important channel of communication. Without the book, you are much more free to make contact with your audience, smile encouragement to a particular child, indicate to another that you have seen some unacceptable behaviour or notice children who have ideas to share.

▶ The words are not fixed

Changing the words when you are reading aloud is normal – and often desirable. With a told story, you have even greater freedom to adapt, elaborate or cut your descriptions according to your audience's response.

▶ The pictures are not predetermined

The illustrations are one of the great virtues of contemporary picture books. Yet it is also vital, and very stimulating, to enable children to create their own mental pictures of a story. Doing this helps develop children's imaginations and gives the storyteller a lot of pleasure.

▶ The story is free for sharing

Storytellers are often rewarded by the love and respect of children. There is no 'expert' author; the story becomes a gift for the child who in turn can keep it in his or her own mind or maybe even retell it to someone else.

Engaging children's attention

One of the arts of storytelling with young children is to remember the kinds of things they enjoy. It is important to build these into your storytelling when you are preparing and presenting your stories.

▶ **Starters**

The following is a story starter typically used by storytellers from the Caribbean.
It depends on the children's enjoyment of being alert and ready to go:
The storyteller asks, "Are you ready?'
When the children say, "Yes,"
the storyteller tests them.
The storyteller says, "Cric!" Without delay, the children must answer, "Crac!"

▶ **Introductions**

Unlike with stories in books, which are frequently introduced by reference to the title, told stories have to be introduced in different ways. One way is to say something about the theme of the story, if possible making a link with your audience and something that they are interested in. Then you can pause and start the story, 'Once upon a time...' Or you could simply get into the story in a more conversational way, moving from talking about it to actually telling it.

▶ **Sounds**

Sounds and sound effects are among the best ways to catch children's attention. You can make sounds with your mouth, for instance, animal noises or atmospheric sounds such as for ghosts or for rain. Musical instruments or a range of objects, such as seeds in a bottle or a piece of wood scratched against a pine-cone, can be used to make a wide variety of other interesting sound effects.

▶ Song

Songs, just as much as rhythms or rhymes, are an important feature of traditional storytelling for children. You can add in familiar little songs where appropriate – for instance, 'Twinkle, twinkle little star' for a night-time story. Or you could make up very simple little songs to go into a story, perhaps as a theme song for a particular character.

▶ Action and gesture

Bodily actions and gestures help focus children's attention and can also help bring them back to the story when their attention has begun to wander. Gestures are useful for communicating all kinds of features from size, for instance of a giant or a pea, to how a character moves or sits. Repeated actions, such as a walking or climbing movement, can ensure that children feel part of the story even when they do not understand all the words.

▶ Expression

Communicating the emotions of a story through facial expressions and bodily postures is a vital part of the storytelling and one thing that distinguishes it from reading aloud. But it is important not to overdo the expression and vital never to frighten young children.

▶ Props

Finding or making suitable props to go with a story can be a highly pleasurable activity. Some props such as a paper mask or a cardboard crown may not be long-lasting. Some may be ideal for follow-on activities where children can make their own versions of what you have created. It is also worth thinking about a 'props box' or a 'props bag' containing a selection of useful cloths and sound-making instruments.

▶ Endings

After finishing your story, a good way to return children to the 'here and now', so to speak, is by using one of the traditional storytelling endings beloved by storytellers in the past. One that children especially enjoy is as follows: 'Snip, snap, snout! My story's told out!'

Creating a good session

What makes a good storytelling session?

Experienced storytellers know the answer is often hard to pin down. Sometimes a story can be told in a completely different way from what was planned – and work! Sometimes a story can fall flat, even when it has worked well before. Sometimes it is the connections between the different elements of a session that make the experience take off.

Range of stories

Over time, if not in every session, it is worth trying to draw on all the three main types of stories.

1. Traditional stories – myths, legends, folktales and fairy tales

These are stories that have been passed on to us by word of mouth, often from very ancient times. In their simplicity of shape and strength of language and situation, they are ideal fare for children.

2. Stories of personal and family experience

All of us have stories, including young children, and they are unique. Yet there are common threads among these stories, and sharing them is one of the most valuable and entertaining things we can do.

3. Newly made-up stories

Even if the storymaker is drawing on known traditional tales or stories of true experience, something fresh is being created each time a new story is made up. Children can feel tremendously involved, and these new stories are unique!

The whole experience

To provide a satisfying experience for the children, a storytelling session needs to cater for a variety of factors.

▶ Variety of material

Apart from stories, other elements that can be included in a storytelling session include simple rhymes or chants and imagination games. Stories from books can also be included alongside a told tale.

▶ Varying levels of participation

Different kinds of participations are a good idea even when sessions are necessarily short because of the children's young age or inexperience. In longer sessions, children also need to be actively involved during some parts of the session even if, in other parts, they may be listening in a quieter way.

▶ Repetition

Unfamiliar material needs to be balanced with things the children already know. Repetition is often a key to their enjoyment: the more they get to know a story, the more they can join in.

▶ A connecting theme

There are a number of ways to link together the different elements of your session:

▷ **Building around the main story you've chosen**

Perhaps your main story is about the sea? Then songs and games can introduce the subject and also sum it up.

▷ **Connecting with a topic you're working on**

Maybe you are working on the topic of Animals or Growing Things? Again the subject provides you with a connecting link for your Storytime.

▷ **Relating to something going on in your setting**

Perhaps your school is having a Book week or building a new playground? Themes like these are worth bearing in mind.

▷ **Linking with seasons or festivals**

Hearing stories connected with the seasons or festivals such as Chinese New Year or Christmas helps children to ground themselves in the world around them.

▶ Follow-up activities

One final way to plan your story session is with a view to follow-on activities:

▷ **Planning to give enough time**

Painting and drawing and craftwork involving making characters from the story, story-mapping – all such activities need time. Plan your session accordingly.

▷ **Planning to provide stimulus**

Follow-on activities can only work if the children want to do them. Plan your session with a view to providing the necessary stimulus for these.

Section 2 – Using chants and rhymes

Twinkle, twinkle, little star

Activity

Make up a new story using the stimulus of a well known nursery rhyme.

Stage 1: **The Nursery Rhyme**

Suggest the children sing the rhyme with you and join in all the usual actions.

> Twinkle, twinkle, little star,
> How I wonder what you are!
> Up above the world so high
> Like a diamond in the sky.
> Twinkle, twinkle, little star,
> How I wonder what you are!

Stage 2: **Making the story**

The story-making proceeds through questions. The children may make various suggestions in reply. If not, quietly suggest some possibilities. Pick up on the most interesting of the children's ideas to lead you through to the next question. It should be just like having a conversation. Pause frequently to encourage their contributions.

I wonder what would happen if we looked up at the sky one night and saw a magic star? ....

Would it look different from all the other stars? ....

Hey – I wonder what would happen if the magic star came down to earth?............

What sound do you think it would make? Perhaps it would make a soft little noise – like WHOOSH?

When the star came down to earth, I wonder where you'd find it? ....

On the grass in the garden? On your pillow when you went to bed?

But I wonder how you'd know the star was magic?........

Would it make other things disappear? Or maybe it would talk to you? ....

I wonder what the magic star would do if you picked it up? Would it make your bedroom disappear? Would it give you a wish?

I wonder where you'd keep your magic star? Would you keep it in a special box? Or in your pocket?

How lucky we would be to have a **Magic Star!**

Follow-up activities

▶ Using plain or coloured paper, cut out enough stars for all the children to have one each.

▶ Invite each child to decorate a star.

▶ Hold a circle time session where the children bring their stars and, if they wish, tell the group a little bit about their own special magic star.

▶ Use a chant to help individual children take turns to talk about their magic star:

> Twinkle, twinkle, little star!
>
> Magic stars are near and far!
>
> Jack is showing us his star!
>
> Please tell us all about it.

▶ Finally hang all the magic stars on a thread or a washing line across the room.

A forest adventure

Activity

Use a chant to create a forest scene that could be the setting for a story. The chant is accompanied by sounds and actions.

The Forest chant

Start a tapping rhythm on your knees as you begin the chant and use hand gestures to suggest the depth and size of the forest. Then throw your arms wide as you invite suggestions of what there may be in the forest.

The forest is deep and the forest is wide
The forest's got lots of things inside.
It's got ... ?

Owls?

Sh! Listen! Let's think of what
sound the owls might be making ...

Too whit ... Too whoo!
Too whit ... Too whoo!

And let's think of an action to show it's owls ... perhaps we could show their big round eyes?

I wonder what else is in the Forest.

The forest is deep and the forest is wide
The forest's got lots of things inside.
It's got owls and ...?

What else?

A snake?

Sh! Listen! Let's think what sound the snake might make ...

Ssssssss...Ssssssss....

And what about an action to show the snake moving along?
Perhaps it's slithering through the grass ...

The forest is deep and the forest is wide
The forest's got lots of things inside.
It's got owls and snakes and...?

So the chant continues, with other creatures or forest features being added at the children's suggestion.

The poor king and his goldfish

Activity
After teaching a less familiar nursery rhyme, follow the rhyme with a story. The rhyme should be accompanied by hand actions to suggest the different creatures, and by sound effects where possible.

The Nursery Rhyme
Verse 1
Wiggle your hand to imitate the movement of a goldfish and bring your hand down towards your toes for the last line.
Make suitable 'surprise' noises at the end of each verse.

The poor king had a goldfish in his bath
A goldfish in his bath, a goldfish in his bath.
The poor king had a goldfish in his bath
And it tickled the poor king's toes.

Verse 2
Make spider movements with your two hands, then step by step make your 'spider hands' crawl up your legs. Exclamations of surprise or horror come at the end.

The poor king had a spider in his shoe
A spider in his shoe, a spider in his shoe.
The poor king had a spider in his shoe
And it crawled right up his leg.

Verse 3
Make the tiger roar and lift up his paws at the end of each line. At the end of the verse, make a big gulping sound.

The poor king had a tiger in his bed
A tiger in his bed, a tiger in his bed.
The poor king had a tiger in his bed
And it swallowed the poor king up.
Umph!

A Follow-up Story: **The Princess Swallowed by a Tiger**

(Developed from the brilliant idea of a little girl at a Sure Start Session in a Wolverhampton Library.)

'What else can I eat?' said the tiger after he'd eaten the king. 'Ah hah! I think I'll eat the princess.'

And that's what the tiger did! He opened his mouth and swallowed the princess in one big gulp.

'Oh dear!' said the people. 'The tiger has swallowed the princess. We'll have to think of a way to get her out!'

So the people thought and thought and wondered what to do.

They came up with all kinds of ideas – perhaps you have got some too?

(wait for children's ideas)

'Let's tickle the tiger,' some people said.
And that is what the people did.

Tickle, tickle, tickle, tickle. They kept on tickling till the tiger started to sneeze.

Uh – uh – uh – uh – uh – SNEEZE!
And when the tiger sneezed,
out came the princess.

Follow-up activities

▶ The story can now repeat itself as the tiger looks round and eats someone else – maybe the prince or the princess' mother. Or maybe the tiger is going to eat all the children listening to this story (in which case it may have to be the children's mothers and fathers who come to get them out).

The ending

The story should probably end with the people hearing a voice calling, 'Help!' The voice is coming out of the tiger and of course, it's the king! The king is still inside the tiger. So the people tickle the tiger again and out comes the king, a little bit cross with his subjects for not remembering about him sooner.

Davey Jones' sailors

Activity

Davey Jones' Sailors is a traditional song. It can either be spoken aloud in rhyme or sung to the well-known tune of 'Bobby Shaftoe'.

What you need:

▶ a big blue cloth and some pebbles and shells help to set the scene.

The Song: **Part One**

Davey Jones had one little sailor
Davey Jones had one little sailor
Davey Jones had one little sailor
One little sailor boy.

(Hold up the little finger of one hand at the beginning of the verse and keep it up throughout.)

He had one, he had two, he had three little sailors.
He had four, he had five, he had six little sailors.
He had seven, he had eight, he had nine little sailors.
Ten little sailor boys.

(Hold up other fingers as appropriate as you go through this verse.)

The Song: **Part Two**

Davey Jones had ten little sailors
Davey Jones had ten little sailors
Davey Jones had ten little sailors
Ten little sailor boys.

(Keep ten fingers held up throughout this verse.)

He had ten, he had nine, he had eight little sailors.
Seven little, six little, five little sailors.
Four, he had three, he had two little sailors,
One little sailor boy.

(Bend down fingers as appropriate until you have one finger left.)

Bringing the song to life

1. Get one volunteer to be Davey Jones and ten other children to be the sailors to act out the song as everyone sings it.
2. Make paper boats, then set down a piece of blue paper or cloth to represent the sea and let the boats sail across it.

Follow-up activities

And how about a story to go with the song?

▶ To set the scene, get the children to help you create the sounds of a storm and a stormy sea (see page 48-49).

The Story

Old Davey Jones was the captain of a ship.
He was planning a special sea journey. So what do you think he needed? ....
Yes, and he needed plenty of sailors.
So Davey Jones went round the town searching for sailors to come and work on his ship.
By the end of the day, he had ten sailors. And the last one he found was just a little boy.

Next day, Davey Jones' ship set sail for the big wide ocean. But when the ship was out at sea, what do you think happened?
Yes, a huge storm blew up with a big strong wind and huge big waves.
Oh dear! One by one, Davey Jones' sailors were washed off the ship by the waves.

In the end, he had just one sailor left – the little sailor boy.

The sailor boy felt sad and started to cry.
But after the waves and the wind calmed down,
what do you think he saw?
All the sailors were swimming back to the ship.
They were shouting and waving. 'Hello! Hello!'
They hadn't been drowned after all!

The little sailor boy helped Davey Jones to throw out a lifebelt.
And one by one, they pulled the sailors back on board.
Then they all had a big celebration.

And that's a good excuse to sing 'Davey Jones' Sailors' one more time:

> Davey Jones had one little sailor
> Davey Jones had one little sailor
> Davey Jones had one little sailor
> One little sailor boy.

He had one, he had two, he had three little sailors.
He had four, he had five, he had six little sailors.
He had seven, he had eight, he had nine little sailors.
Ten little sailor boys.

> Davey Jones had ten little sailors
> Davey Jones had ten little sailors
> Davey Jones had ten little sailors
> Ten little sailor boys.

He had ten, he had nine,
He had eight little sailors.
Seven little, six little,
five little sailors.
Four, he had three,
He had two little sailors,
One little sailor boy.

Going for a story walk

Activity

Create a story with the children around a story walk chant that suggests you're going to visit different places. As you say the chant, make a walking rhythm with your hands. One way is by cupping your two hands over your knees, then moving each in turn high into the air above your knee, then back.

Introduction

Invite the children to come on a Story Walk.
Make it sound exciting – I wonder where we'll go?

The story walk rhythm

First establish the walking rhythm, then soon after begin the story walk chant:

Walking, walking...
Let's go walking...
Out of the door...
And down the road...

I wonder where we'll go.
To the park?
OK ... Here we go ...

Walking, walking...
Let's go walking...
Out of the door...
And down the road...

We've come to the park...
Let's have a look...
I wonder what we'll see?

Cup your fingers round your eyes as if you've got your specs on!

The duck pond?

> Walking, walking...
> Let's go walking...

We've come to the duck pond...
What can we see?
Quacking noises here!

> Ducks!

And where else shall we go
in the park?
To the roundabout?

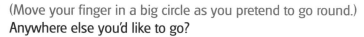

> Walking, walking...
> Let's go walking...

We've come to the roundabout.
Shall we have a go?

(Move your finger in a big circle as you pretend to go round.)
Anywhere else you'd like to go?

Options

It's up to you and the children where you go – somewhere else in the park? To the shops? The swimming pool? Into the woods? The journey can take you wherever the children suggest, but it should always end with going home.

Coming home chant

Down the road...
In through the door...
Now we are at home again...
Let's have a cup of tea!

The far-away story walk

Options

A journey to the seaside? A magic castle? A forest in a faraway land? The moon?

Preparation

It's a good idea to think about the options in advance so you are ready for the possibilities. What might you and the children see? Waves splashing onto the shore ... a giant who lives in the magic castle ... tigers roaring in the forest ... the man in the moon saying hello ...?

The far-away story walk chant

The pattern of the walk is the same as for the story walk on page 24. But it has a different chant.

Walking, walking,
Let's go walking ...
A week and a month and a year and a day...
Let's go somewhere far away!

Follow-up activities

▶ Create different scenes in different parts of the room – a farm, a river, a jungle, a castle. Make big footprints to go on the floor to take you between the different scenes.
Draw your story walk on a huge piece of paper. The line you draw is the path of the story. Different parts of the paper can represent different destinations and the children can be invited to add to the drawing some of the things they'd like to see.

Wiggle-Woof and Waggle-Woof

Activity

A new version of a well-known action chant for young children. Your two hands represent two dogs, Wiggle-Woof and Waggle-Woof. Your thumb shows each dog begging. Your little finger is the tail.

The story has an introduction and three sections

1. One day, Wiggle-Woof goes to visit Waggle-Woof.
2. Next day, Waggle-Woof goes to visit Wiggle-Woof.
3. On the third day, they meet in the middle.

Introduction

Wiggle-Woof is a little brown dog. He belongs to Mrs Wiggle.
Here he is sitting up to beg. Here he is wagging his tail.
Wiggle-Woof has a friend called Waggle-Woof.
Waggle-Woof is a spotty dog. She belongs to Mrs Waggle.
Here she is sitting up to beg. Here she is wagging her tail.
This is a story about them.

Section 1

One day, Wiggle-Woof decided to go for a walk after breakfast.
He wanted to go and see his friend.
So he went out through his dog-flap and waggled his tail.
Then he set off to Waggle-Woof's house.
Up the hill ... woof
Down the hill ...woof
Up the hill ... woof
Down the hill ...woof
Up the hill ... woof
Down the hill ... woof
... until he got to Mrs Waggle's.

There he barked at the gate. Woof Woof!
But no one came.
Mrs Waggle didn't come.
Waggle-Woof didn't come.

So Wiggle-Woof barked again. Woof Woof! Woof Woof!

But no one came. So Wiggle-Woof ran home.

Up the hill ... woof
Down the hill ...woof
Up the hill ... woof
Down the hill ...woof
Up the hill ... woof
Down the hill ... woof
...until he got to Mrs Wiggle's.

When he got home, he went in through his dog-flap.
'Where have you been, Wiggle-Woof?' said Mrs Wiggle.
But all Wiggle-Woof said was, 'Woof!'
Then Mrs Wiggle gave him a biscuit.

Section 2

The next day, Waggle-Woof decided to go for a walk after
breakfast. She wanted to go and see her friend. So she went out
through her dog-flap and waggled her tail.

Then she set off.
Up the hill ... woof
Down the hill ...woof
Up the hill ... woof
Down the hill ...woof
Up the hill ... woof
Down the hill ... woof
... until she got to Mrs Wiggle's house.

There she barked at the gate.
Woof Woof!
But no one came.
Mrs Wiggle didn't come.
Wiggle-Woof didn't come.
So Waggle-Woof barked again. Woof Woof! Woof Woof!

But no one came.
So Waggle-Woof ran home.
Up the hill ... woof
Down the hill ...woof
Up the hill ... woof
Down the hill ...woof
Up the hill ... woof
Down the hill ... woof
...until she got to Mrs Waggle's.

When she got home, she went in through her dog-flap.
'Where have you been, Waggle-Woof?' said Mrs Waggle.

But all Waggle-Woof said was 'Woof!'
Then Mrs Waggle gave her a biscuit.

Section 3

The next day what do you think happened?

Mrs Wiggle and Mrs Waggle got on their mobile phones and
decided to meet up for a walk together.
'Let's bring our dogs,' they said, 'and we'll meet in the middle.'

So Mrs Wiggle put Wiggle-Woof on his lead.
Mrs Waggle put Waggle-Woof on her lead.
And off they went.
Up the hill ... woof
Down the hill ...woof
Up the hill ... woof

And that's where they met – in the field
at the top of the hill in the middle!

'Hello,' said Mrs Wiggle.
'Hello,' said Mrs Waggle.
'Woof-woof,' said Wiggle-Woof.
'Woof-woof,' said Waggle-Woof.

Then Mrs Wiggle and Mrs Waggle unfastened the dog leads and Wiggle-Woof and Waggle-Woof chased each other round until it was time to go home.

'Wiggle-Woof,' called Mrs Wiggle.
'Waggle-Woof,' called Mrs Waggle.

At first, Wiggle-Woof and Waggle-Woof didn't come. They were too busy exploring the field.

But in the end they did come back.
So Mrs Wiggle and Mrs Waggle put their leads on them and took them home.

Down the hill ... woof
Up the hill ... woof
Down the hill ... woof

When they got home, Mrs Wiggle and Wiggle-Woof went in through their front door.
And Mrs Waggle and Waggle-Woof went in through their front door.

Then the two ladies had nice cups of tea and the two dogs had a biscuit and a drink of water.

And that's the end of the story.

Flossie the flea takes a trip

Activity

You are telling – and drawing – the story of a flea making a journey around a cat's head. At the beginning, it's not clear what the journey is about. By the end it should be obvious! You may want to practise drawing this story first.

Preparation

You need a sheet of paper and a pencil or, if you like, some coloured crayons. If you're going to tell the story to a large group, pin the paper onto an easel so everyone can see. If you have just a few children around you, you could keep the paper on a table or your lap.

The story

Once there was a flea called Flossie and one day she went on holiday – to a very interesting place.

First she saw a mountain.
Start drawing the cat's face: a downstroke with your pencil represents the mountain – the cat's nose!

At the bottom of the mountain were two dark caves.
Add two dots at the base of your downstroke – the cat's nostrils!

Beside each cave grew tall wavy reeds.
Draw in two sets of thin lines – the cat's whiskers!

And not far from the mountain were two blue lakes, one each side of the mountain.
Add two circles with dots in the middle – the cat's eyes!

The first day of her holiday, Flossie the Flea decided to go on a trip.
Start to draw Flossie's journey at a point directly above the long low mountain.

Your pencil now makes a pointed cat's ear.

First she came to a steep little hill. She climbed the hill – Hoppity hop! – and – Wheeee! - slid down the other side.

A long curving line brings you down to the cat's chin!

Next Flossie followed a path that curved past a round blue lake with an island in the middle, past the long low mountain and a small dark cave and underneath the tall wavy reeds.

A matching curve brings you up the other side of the cat's face!

After a while, the path started curving back the other way – and soon she was going underneath more tall wavy reeds, past another cave and that long low mountain, past another lake with an island in the middle.

You're now reaching the cat's other ear.

Suddenly she came to another steep hill just like the one at the start of her journey. She climbed the hill – Hoppity hop! – and – Wheeee! – she slid down the other side.

You're nearly home!

Suddenly Flo realised she was nearly back where she started. With one last hop she was there!

Phew!

Do you know where Flossie the Flea had been? Yes, she'd jumped up onto a cat. And her special holiday trip had taken her all the way round the cat's head.

Section 4 – Make a story

Using an object

Activity

Bring along an interesting object to stimulate story ideas. The activity need last only a couple of minutes but could take off and last for weeks. Success probably depends on the object itself and thinking beforehand about questions to stimulate interest. It will further intrigue the children if the object isn't fully visible at first but wrapped up in paper or cloth, or hidden in a box or bag.

Here are some examples:

A key

Keys invariably have a sense of mystery about them. They make us wonder. What doors or boxes do they open? What lies beyond or inside? Choose a nice big heavy key. Or maybe a very tiny one. As you look at it with the children, you can start your questions.

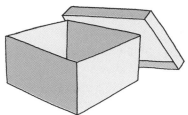

What door might this key open?
Who owns the door? Who keeps the key?
What could be behind the door?
Or maybe the key is for a box?
Has the box got a secret inside?

A cardboard box

Cardboard boxes come in all shapes and sizes. Will you choose a huge one? Or one with words such as HANDLE WITH CARE? You could bring your choice to Storytime, put it down beside you, then start talking about it. Or how about leaving it somewhere in the room, then at Storytime pointing it out and asking the children about it?

Might there be someone who lives in the box?
A little creature?
Does it ever come out, this creature?
Where does it go?
What does it look like? Why don't we ever see it?
What does it think of us?

A special shoe

Magic shoes often crop up in stories. But shoes are familiar things as well. Remember your first pair of shoes? Or buying that special pair for a special occasion? Bring along an interesting looking example from home or a jumble sale. Let the children have a look, then begin the thinking.

What would happen if the shoe were magic?
Might it make someone disappear?
Or jump up very high?
What if the shoe were left on the street and
someone came and tried it on?
What would happen to that person?

A hat

Hats express character and purpose. We use them for all kinds of reasons – staying warm, looking smart, keeping hair out of the way, expressing the fact of belonging to the same school or club. Bring along a couple of hats. But instead of wondering if they are magic, try thinking what real people might wear them.

Would it be an old lady? Or someone going out in the snow?
Where does the hat get kept at home?
What might happen when the person goes
out in the hat?
What if it blows off?
Or what if the person gives it to a snowman?

Follow-up activities

▶ Just passing round an object for children to examine can be very productive – for language and imagination, concentration and learning to take turns.How about a shell, stick or pebble you've picked up from a beach? Or a special glove puppet or toy? When you've used a toy such as a frog or teddy bear as a prop to start a story, passing it from child to child can be a satisfying way to end your Storytime, giving the children the chance to handle and talk about the prop you've used.

Using a familiar theme

Activity

Picking a familiar story theme provides an excellent basis for a new story. One of the most common is getting lost and then getting found. Take this as your basic idea. But it not only provides you with the basic pattern of your story, it can help you feel that you as the storyteller won't get lost in your storymaking as the end of the story is obvious!

Here is an example:

The kitten that wandered away

Set the scene by talking about a mother cat that has a litter of kittens. Describe the cat – what colour? what personality? – and say a bit about the kittens.

Describe how the cat looks after her kittens and how the children in the household love each one of them.

Then, with a slight change of voice, make the story move into what happens one particular evening. Maybe the kittens have grown quite a lot bigger and more adventurous by the time of this particular event. Maybe the kitchen door happens to have been left open. Describe how one of the kittens wanders out of the door, wondering what is to be found outside it. Of course, identify which of the kittens this is and describe the kitten's feelings and thoughts (as if it was a human being!)

Perhaps make the kitten experience some of the frightening encounters that a garden at night could provide.

For example, there might be wind blowing in the bushes and the kitten might be frightened at the sound. Or there might be a dog sniffing around the lawn in the garden next door. The kitten may hear it snuffling, then barking.

Or there might be a plastic bag blowing about in the garden and again the kitten might be frightened, thinking it is a huge big bird or a monster. After making up a few examples (and using some good sound effects to make them come to life), you could then reveal that the kitten feels thoroughly lost.

Now is the time for the rescue. You could describe the children of the household getting very worried when they realise that one of their kittens is lost. Then you could describe them searching for the lost kitten. Or you could get the kitten's mother looking around the kitchen, sniffing here and there to try and find her kitten. Or the children's father or mother might join in the search.

Whatever option you choose, the kitten is obviously going to be found in the end and brought back into the house with enormous relief and a great deal of gladness.

Follow-up activities

Objects that get lost and found can also form the basis of good simple stories. After all, the situation is very familiar – children (and adults!) lose things all the time:

▶ So you could echo the common human experience by making up a story about a lost toy, and the pleasure of when it finally turns up.

▶ Or you could base the story you tell around an experience that has actually happened to you – losing a ring or temporarily losing a child. Maybe your listeners will be reminded of something that has happened to them and want to tell their stories too.

Using a puppet or toy

Activity

A well-chosen puppet or soft toy can become the much-loved hero or heroine in a long-running series of stories. If experience is anything to go by, these stories will probably be remembered by children in your group many, many years later. Lots of fathers (and it's often fathers!) make the idea the basis of their bedtime storytelling. It can work equally well in Storytime in school.

Here is an example:

Miranda the marvellous mermaid

Suppose you have an attractive mermaid puppet. Give the character a name (which the children might help choose) and she can start developing a whole world around herself and a life full of adventures.

One episode could involve Miranda in finding a friend. Maybe she starts off feeling lonely. Then perhaps she can come across a very fine fish – or another mermaid - who shows her wonderful underwater places, rocks and caves and seaweed gardens. Or maybe there's a girl or boy who regularly comes swimming at the beach on that part of the coast where Miranda lives. Whatever option you choose, there is plenty to talk about in describing Miranda's encounter with her new friend, the development and consolidation of the friendship and maybe some kind of celebration.

Another episode could involve Miranda in finding a new home.
Maybe she chooses an underwater cave or perhaps a shipwrecked boat on the bottom of the ocean. Again, whatever the option, there is plenty to describe as she arranges her home, chooses special things to decorate it and makes it comfortable.

When everything is organised, there could be another party.

Stories of mermaids often involve helping a human being. You could echo this particular theme by choosing for your story a child who gets into trouble on the rocks or a fisherman in trouble out at sea. Perhaps in the case of the fisherman, a violent storm is gathering out on the ocean and Miranda the mermaid warns him and leads him home to safety through the waves.

Dozens more adventures can ensue. Miranda could suffer some kind of accident. Or she could find a beautiful ring at the bottom of the sea. Or she could wish to have a smart new jacket or a different hairstyle. If the character proves popular, the series can run and run (or swim and swim!)

Follow-up activities

Successful characters for a long-running series of stories could include:

▶ a human character (a rag-doll or clown)

▶ an animal character (a bear, monkey or whatever appeals)

The stories can pick up on suggestions from the children and can allow plenty of opportunity for other activities such as:

▶ a mapping out where the character lives

▶ making paintings or drawings of the story

▶ creating props for the character's world

▶ reading related picture books.

Using an actual event

Activity

Basing a story on an actual event that has occurred in your class can prove engaging for your listeners and sometimes very instructive. It could even help you to sort out some of those typical classroom problems. But don't reveal that you are telling a true story of something that actually happened. Change the names of the people concerned or don't use specific names at all. Involve the children by asking them at various stages what they think might have happened next.

Here is an example:

The boy who wore glasses

Maybe you've got in your class a child who wears glasses and who has been bullied a bit because of it? After all, this is a very common occurrence!

Start your story by talking about a little boy who learns he has to wear glasses. You can describe the different feelings that this little boy has and you could involve your listeners in thinking about it too.

Bring out the little boy's fears and describe, maybe, how his mother and father try to reassure him. Talk about how the glasses may help him – what do your listeners think?

Describe the little boy going to school in his glasses for the first time. Talk about what he imagines other people are thinking and saying. Ask your listeners what they think might happen.

Move on to talk about how there is one bigger boy who laughs at the child with glasses and starts to call him names. Maybe the children know what sort of names the bigger boy uses – Four-Eyes, maybe?

Talk about how the name-calling continues and the little boy gets more and more upset until one day, maybe, he comes into the classroom crying. Describe how one of the other children, or maybe the little boy's teacher, tries to find out what's wrong.

What do your listeners think might happen? Draw on your own experience by describing how the teacher handles the situation, perhaps talking to the little boy on his own, then talking to the children as a group about glasses and why people need to wear them.

Maybe in your story the teacher then decides to comment on the whole episode by telling the children a story? Maybe it's exactly the story you've just told your listeners now?

Follow-up activities

▶ Perhaps there is a child in your class whose mother is having a new baby?

▶ Or maybe there is someone who will be going into hospital for an operation?

▶ Or perhaps the children are coming to the end of the year and thinking about moving to a new class next year?

All these sorts of situations may give you the idea for a series of stories which in turn help your listeners to recognise and understand their own and other children's experiences.

Important – it is essential that stories of this type are not associated with the circumstances of any particular child or children in your group or class.

Section 5 – True stories:

A tale of your own

Activity

Tell a story from your own personal experience. The story could be something that has happened to you or to someone in your family or a friend or something you were told by someone you met.

Preparation

1. Choosing a story

To help yourself find a story to tell, run your mind over some different themes:

▶ cats, dogs or other pets you have had

▶ special journeys you have made

▶ funny things that have happened to you, perhaps when you were a child

▶ special people in your life such as a favourite Grandad, Granny, Aunty or Uncle

▶ a place where you used to live

Try matching the story you choose to a theme you are working on with the children at the time:

▶ a frog story at tadpole time

▶ a Christmas story when it's coming up to Christmas

▶ something about you as a child when the theme is 'Ourselves'

2. Getting ready to tell your story

Simplify the story down to the basics of what happened and in what order.
For example:
We heard a funny noise coming from the kitchen.
When we tracked it down, we saw that the
kitten had got into a wide-bottomed
jug on the window-sill and was
whizzing round and round inside,
chasing his own tail.

Ask yourself if you could add dialogue.
For example: 'What's that funny noise in the kitchen?'
'Sounds like a machine gone mad!'

See if it is appropriate to add some sound-effects.
For example: It was a funny sort of noise, like this – zzzzzzzzz

Perhaps gestures could help bring the story to life?
For example: Point your finger upwards and whirl it round and round to suggest
the kitten in the jug.

Think how you are going to introduce your story.
For example: Have you ever heard of a cat chasing its tail?
Well, I'll tell you what happened one day when my cat tried catching his own tail.

3. Telling your story

▶ Recount the story as simply and
   naturally as possible.

▶ Allow plenty of pauses for the
   children to take it in.

▶ Some interesting detail (not too
   much!) allows the children to
   savour the scene.

Make plenty of time at the end for the children
to talk about it with you. They will also probably want to mention similar things
in their own experience. Remember it's your story – you are giving something of
yourself and your audience will
appreciate that.

Involving the children

Activity

Organise a story-sharing session in which the children become the storytellers. The basic idea of a story-sharing session is to let the children realise that they have stories of their own and to give them an opportunity to share their stories with the group. Even three-year-olds and four-year-olds can surprise you with their storytelling ability.

Preparation

Stage 1

The storyteller's rule of thumb is that, to get a story, you must give one first. So the first step is to decide on the story you're going to tell to start the story sharing. Is there going to be a theme such as Pets or Going on a Journey or Losing Things?

Stage 2

Decide on the story-sharing method you're going to use.

Option A

After telling your story, you invite children to think if they've got any stories of their own that are like it and to put their hands up if they have. Then you ask children one by one to come out to tell their story to the others.

Option B

After telling your story, you invite children to choose a friend to talk to. Then let them sit in pairs to see if they can tell their stories to each other. After a few minutes, call them back to the whole group, maybe into a circle, to share their stories.

The Story Sharing Session

Think about how to organise the session

The children could sit in a group or in a circle.
Have a 'story chair' ready beside yours for any child that wants to sit down to tell their story.

Introduce a chant between children's stories

A chant gives children confidence and a sense of fun. It also gives something for the children to join in with as they tap their hands on their knees in rhythm with the words.

Example:

> All of us are storytellers!
> All of us are storytellers!
> Some of us are boys, some of us are girls.
> But all of us are storytellers.
> Sh! Sh! Sh!

There are many ways to ring the changes on this simple chant:
> Some of us are tall, some of us are short.
> Some of us are old, some of us are young.

Help the children to develop their stories

1. Make sure the children are given time to hear and understand each others' stories.
   Example:
   A little girl tells a story about how her two gerbils got loose one day. When the gerbils were found, they were in the wardrobe in the parents' bedroom – chewing on the make-up that the mother of the family kept on one of the wardrobe shelves.

2. Go over the story in an informal way after it has been told, asking the storyteller any relevant questions.

   Example:
   How did the gerbils get out of their cage? Was there a terrible mess? What did your mother say?

3. Develop the story informally by raising some of the hidden questions and possibilities.

Example:
How could the gerbils have got out of their cage?
How did they get into the wardrobe?
Wouldn't it have been funny if the gerbils had put the make-up on themselves?

Follow-up activities

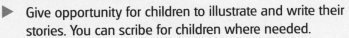

► Give opportunity for children to illustrate and write their stories. You can scribe for children where needed.

► Help children to record their stories. They will love to listen to them afterwards.

Musical stories

Activity

A range of musical instruments can create magical effects which bring a story to life. They can also help children who do not or cannot speak by providing valuable ways for them to contribute. Atmospheres can be created, specific sounds suggested.

Preparation

A good start is to review the instruments you have available, experimenting to see what sounds they can suggest.

You may want to look out for some new instruments:

an ocean drum
– for the sound of the sea or waves on beaches

a rain stick
– for the sound of rain or hot, wet jungly places or a waterfall

a set of bells
– for all magical transformations, such as the appearance of fairies

a xylophone
– for characters flying through the air or climbing the stairs

a drum
– for announcing that things are about to change

a kyamba
– an East African instrument also suggesting rain or sea

You may also want to experiment with other sound-making objects:

- ▶ a bottle you could blow into to create the sound of the wind
- ▶ beans in a tin for things rattling about
- ▶ a heavy chain to rattle for spooky occasions
- ▶ a pair of shells that can be tapped together to summon up a galloping horse
- ▶ a bowl of water to make splashing sounds
- ▶ a piece of wood scratched against a pine cone for little creatures in the forest.

Creating a sound-story with your instruments

When you've selected a range of instruments and other objects – and especially if there's another adult to help you – you can easily create a sound-story without words.

Try asking the children to sit in a circle with their eyes closed. Then start playing your instruments, ranging them so that you build up the sounds, then gradually getting quieter again. Of course, the children will probably peep – but the exercise can be built on so that they really start to listen.

Afterwards, see if the children have any thoughts about what was going on. They may just want to talk about the kinds of sounds the instruments made, but that's the first step towards a sound-story.

Follow-up activities

- ▶ If you have time, try recording your sounds, then playing it to the children. What will they make of the sounds?
- ▶ Next time you tell a story, ask the children when you have finished what sounds could be used to bring the words to life. Share out the instruments and let the children try them out as you tell the story again. You will need to 'conduct' the music, bringing the children in and signalling them to stop.

Sound and movement

Activity

Sound effects and actions can help evoke different atmospheres and suggest different weathers and landscapes. They are vital ingredients for helping children to participate in stories, making them feel they are right there in the stories themselves. They are especially important for children with special needs who find it difficult to join in for one reason or another, and for second-language speakers.

Here are some examples:

Creating a storm

The storm begins with the sounds of gradually increasing wind. Thunder and lightning herald the start of the rain. After a while, the storm dies gradually away. Calm returns.

The wind

Start the wind with a light blowing sound. Gradually introduce sh-shing sounds and the noise of wind moaning or howling to make the wind more intense.
Swaying your body and moving your arms from side to side helps to summon up the effect.

The rain

The first big drops of rain are made with your hands held high in the air, fingers of each hand clicking alternately. Then when the majority of children have joined in, start tapping two fingers of one hand against the palm of the other. Again when most have taken up the theme, start tapping your hands on your knees. Finally move to drumming your feet on the floor. To make the rain stop, go through all these actions again in reverse sequence.

Lightning

Hold both your hands on your lap in readiness. Then, making an 'electric' sort of sound, suddenly raise them both in the air. It's wise to warn the children in advance that this is going to sound quite scary!

Thunder

Raise one fist high in the air in preparation and, as you bring it down onto your knee, making a booming sound with your mouth. Continue with alternate fists to give four or five booming sounds of thunder. Again, warn the children that this is going to be loud!

Creating a seascape

The waves of the sea coming in to shore can be suggested by movements of your arms combined with sound effects.

Leaning slightly backwards and sucking your breath in with a hissing sound, draw each arm towards your chest in turn in circular motions to give the sense of a wave building up.

For the waves to break on the shore, lean outwards slightly, increasing the speed and strength of your circular arm movements as you now change to making a splashing sound.

Creating a forest scene

A forest can be suggested by each person in the group making the shape of a tree. Sound effects can be added.

Give the sense of the tree shape by holding your arms up together in front of you, hands and fingers splayed outwards. If all the children make individual trees it creates the sense of a forest.

Make the trees sway in the wind – gently to give the sense of a summer day, more violently to make a winter storm. Populate the forest with the sounds of birds – owls or parrots depending on the geography.

The gingerbread man

Activity

Tell a well-known story – without the aid of the book!

The Gingerbread Man

This is a story most of us remember – more or less! Check out any bits you've forgotten by reading through the version below. Or look up one or two of your favourite book versions. Refer to pages 68-69 if you want help with some basic ways of remembering a story.

The basic plot

A gingerbread man jumps down on the floor and runs away. The old woman who has made him runs after.

First he passes a cow. The cow wants to eat him and runs after him. Then he passes a horse. The horse wants to eat him and runs after him.

Next he passes a farmer. The farmer wants to eat him and runs after him.

Now he comes to a fox. The fox wants to eat him but pretends that he doesn't.

The fox offers to give the gingerbread man a ride across the river. On the way, the gingerbread man has to climb nearer and nearer the fox's mouth. Then the fox starts to eat him and soon he is all gone.

Remember the song

The song is sung with a la-la lilt. Sometimes, to get children joining in, it helps to wave your arm from side to side like a conductor as you sing.

> Run, run as fast as you can
> You can't catch me!
> I'm the gingerbread man.

The story

There was once a little old woman and a little old man who didn't have any children. One day the little old woman made a gingerbread man. She put raisins for his eyes and raisins for his buttons and she gave him a nice smiling face. Then she put him in the oven to cook.

When the little old woman opened the oven to see if the ginger bread man was ready, the little gingerbread man jumped out of the oven and onto the floor. Then he ran out of the door, down the path and off down the road. And as he went, the little old woman and the little old man ran after him calling, 'Come back, come back, little gingerbread man.'

But the little gingerbread man ran on and as he went he sang:

> Run, run as fast as you can
> You can't catch me!
> I'm the gingerbread man.

Down the road, the little gingerbread man went past a field. In the field was a cow and when the cow saw the gingerbread man, she thought he looked very tasty. The cow called out, 'Come here, little gingerbread man. I want to eat you up.'

But the little gingerbread man called back, 'I've run away from a little old woman. And I've run away from a little old man. And I can run away from you, I can, I can.'

> Run, run as fast as you can
> You can't catch me!
> I'm the gingerbread man.

The little gingerbread man ran on. And the cow ran after along with the little old woman and the little old man.

Soon the little gingerbread man went past a horse. The horse called out, 'Come here, little gingerbread man. I want to eat you up.'

But the little gingerbread man called back, 'I've run away from a cow and I've run away from a little old woman and a little old man. And I can run away from you, I can, I can.'

> Run, run as fast as you can
> You can't catch me!
> I'm the gingerbread man.

The little gingerbread man ran on.
And the horse ran after along
with the cow, the little old woman
and the little old man.

Next the little gingerbread man passed a farmer working in the fields. The farmer called out, 'Come here, little gingerbread man. I want to eat you up.'

But the little gingerbread man called back, 'I've run away from a horse and a cow and a little old woman and a little old man. And I can run away from you, I can, I can.'

> Run, run as fast as you can
> You can't catch me!
> I'm the gingerbread man.

The little gingerbread man ran on and the farmer ran after him along with the horse and the cow and the little old woman and the little old man.

Next the little gingerbread man passed a fox and the fox was feeling very hungry. But the fox was cunning. He just said to the gingerbread man, 'You're all right with me, little gingerbread man. I wouldn't dream of eating you up.'

Then – oh dear! – the little gingerbread man came to a river. What was he going to do? He had to get across the river because all those people were chasing him and they all wanted to eat him up. But the little gingerbread man couldn't swim!

Suddenly the fox came up beside the little gingerbread man. 'I'll take you across the river, little gingerbread man,' said the fox. 'Just jump on my tail and I'll swim you across.' So the little gingerbread man jumped onto the fox's tail as the fox jumped in the river and started swimming across. But soon the little gingerbread man was getting wet.

'Climb up onto my back,' said the wily fox. 'Then you won't get wet.' So the little gingerbread man jumped onto the fox's back. But he was still getting wet.

'Jump up onto my nose,' said the greedy fox. 'Then you won't get wet.'

So the little gingerbread man jumped onto the fox's nose. But just as they reached the other side of the river, the fox threw back his head and opened his jaws - SNAP! – and ate some of the little gingerbread man.

'Oh dear,' said the little gingerbread man.
'I'm half gone.'

SNAP! went the fox again.
'Oh dear,' said the little gingerbread man. 'I'm three-quarters gone.'

SNAP! went the fox one last time. And that was the end of the little gingerbread man.

Follow-up activities

▶ Cook gingerbread men with the children.

▶ Make cut-out gingerbread men from card and glue a stick to the back of each so the children can hold them up and move them about as you tell the story.

▶ Draw a long curvy path down a long piece of paper so the children can fill in the story, drawing in the various characters and scenes or playing with small world figures.

The cat sat on the mat

This story has been developed for telling from the idea of 'Cat on the Mat' by Brian Wildsmith.

Activity

Tell a cumulative story with a basic repetitive pattern which adds characters as it progresses. Sound effects are repeated again and again and more new characters can be added at the children's suggestion.

Story summary

As the cat sleeps on the mat, other animals come and join her. The cat either does not see them or pretends not to notice. The animals get bigger and bigger. The twist in the tail arrives when the cat's traditional enemy arrives – a little mouse.

The Story

The cat sat on the mat. She didn't move. Was she fast asleep? Then the door opened and a dog came in.

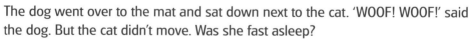

The dog went over to the mat and sat down next to the cat. 'WOOF! WOOF!' said the dog. But the cat didn't move. Was she fast asleep?

The door opened again and a pig came in. The pig went over to the mat and sat down next to the dog. 'OINK! OINK!' grunted the pig. 'WOOF! WOOF!' barked the dog.

But the cat didn't move. Was she fast asleep? Then the door opened once more and a cow came in. The cow went over to the mat and sat down next to the pig.

'MOO! MOO!' mooed the cow.
'OINK! OINK!' grunted the pig.
'WOOF! WOOF!' barked the dog. But the cat didn't move. Was she fast asleep?

The door opened again and a horse came in.
The horse went over to the mat and sat down next to the cow.

'NEIGH! NEIGH!' neighed the horse.
'MOO! MOO!' mooed the cow.
'OINK! OINK!' grunted the pig.
'WOOF! WOOF!' barked the dog.

But the cat didn't move. Was she fast asleep?

Then the door opened and an elephant came in.
The elephant went over to the mat and sat
down next to the horse.
'EEE! EEE!' trumpeted the elephant.
'NEIGH! NEIGH!' neighed the horse.
'MOO! MOO!' mooed the cow.
'OINK! OINK!' grunted the pig.
'WOOF! WOOF!' barked the dog.
But the cat didn't move. Was she fast asleep?

Then the door opened again, very quietly, and a tiny little mouse came in.
The mouse went over to the mat and found
a tiny little space next to the elephant.
'EEK! EEK!' squeaked the mouse.

The cat pricked up her ears and
opened her eyes, stood up and stretched, did a great big MIAOW! and chased the
mouse and all the other creatures straight towards the door.

'EEK! EEK! squeeked the mouse.
'EEE! EEE!' trumpeted the elephant.
'NEIGH! NEIGH!' neighed the horse.
'MOO! MOO!' mooed the cow.
'OINK! OINK!' grunted the pig.
'WOOF! WOOF!' barked the dog.

They all ran out of the door as fast as they could and after they'd all gone, the cat went back to the mat and sat down. She closed her eyes and very soon, she really was fast asleep.

Follow-up activities

▶ Try telling the story with a set of animal figures as props. Afterwards, set up the animal figures on a table or on a mat on the floor for the children to play with.

The three wishes

This is a traditional European story. There are different versions, but this is the most common.

The basic story

An old man and an old woman live together, very contented but very poor. One day the old woman finds a fairy in the garden and the fairy says she can have three wishes. The old woman is very excited.

That evening, the old woman is talking with her husband about what wishes they could choose. But as she starts making their supper, she sees there isn't much food. Without thinking, she wishes they had a nice fat sausage.

Suddenly, there's the sausage – in the middle of the frying pan.

One wish has been used up! Crossly the old man says he wishes the sausage was on his wife's nose. Suddenly, it is. Two wishes have been used up.

Now what are they going to do with their third wish? Ask for lots of money? But what about the wife's sausage-nose? The husband has a suggestion: if they have lots of money, they could make a gold cover to put over her sausage-nose.

The old woman is horrified. The two of them argue and argue and get crosser and crosser until eventually they decide to use their third wish to make everything go back to how it was before.

Preparing the story

Some ways of remembering a story can be found on pages 67/68.

You could also make a word skeleton like this

old woman ... old man ...
fairy ... three wishes ...
supper ... sausage ...
nose ... next ...
back to normal

Scenes to visualise could include

▶ the fairy in the garden (or somewhere else)
  – what does the fairy look like?
  – has the fairy got wings?
  – does she make a magic sound?
  – how does the old woman react when she sees her?

▶ the old couple's kitchen
  – is there an armchair where the old man sits?
  – does the old woman cook over the fire or on a stove?
  – what had she got for supper - just a few potatoes to fry?

▶ the sausage
  – what does the sausage look like sizzling in the frying pan?
  – what does it look like on the old woman's nose?

▶ the argument
  – what do the old people say to each other? You silly old woman?
  You silly old man?

Follow-up activities

▶ Talking about wishes is a natural follow-on. What would
you choose if you were given a magic wish? Could you paint
a picture of your wish? Or cut pictures out of magazines or
catalogues of different things that people might want? Perhaps there
could be a magic wish box with everyone's wishes in it.

The hat seller and the monkeys

This story comes from India, where many versions exist. These give scope to you as storyteller to pick and choose the way you want to present some aspects of the story.

The basic plot

A hat seller makes hats for selling and goes about selling them from place to place. One day he (or she) is on his way through a forest. Tired and hungry, he sits down to eat his lunch, then he goes off to sleep. While he is asleep, monkeys come down from the trees and take his hats. When he wakes up, he sees the monkeys up the trees, all wearing his hats, and he has to try to get his hats back from them. After a lot of effort, he succeeds and hurries on his way.

Choices

The hat seller could be:

- ▶ old or young
- ▶ female or male
- ▶ witty or a bit slow-minded

The hat seller could take his hats from place to place by:

- ▶ piling them all on his head
- ▶ carrying them in a bag
- ▶ wheeling them along in a hand-cart

The hat seller's lunch could be:

- ▶ samosas and fruit
- ▶ sandwiches and crisps
- ▶ anything the listeners suggest

There could be a hat seller's chant:

> Hats for sale! Hats for sale!
> Big hats, small hats,
> Red hats, blue hats,
> Hats for weddings,
> Hats for school,
> Hats for sale! Hats for sale!

The hat seller could try getting his hats back by:

- ▶ pleading with the monkeys
- ▶ ordering the monkeys to give them back
- ▶ asking for his hats in different languages.

The story

Once there was a man who made hats – all kinds of hats, all colours of hats, hats for all kinds of people.

One day the hat seller was going through a forest. He was on his way to town to sell the hats he'd made. But the day was hot, the way was long, and soon the hat seller felt very tired.

'I'll sit down and have my lunch,' thought the hat seller. And that is what he did.

When he'd finished eating, the hat seller leaned back against a big tall tree, pulled his own hat over his eyes, and went fast asleep.

While he was sleeping, as you'd have heard if you'd been there, there was a chattering noise from the branches above. It was monkeys ... monkeys peering down at the hat seller and looking with interest at his basket of hats.

Quickly, quietly, the monkeys crept down from the trees, put their paws in the hat seller's basket and took out all of his hats. Then they put the hats on their heads and crept back into the trees.

When the hat seller woke up, he heard the monkeys chattering. The noise sounded just like laughing. And when the hat seller looked up in the trees, he saw the monkeys wearing his hats. How furious he was!

'Give me back my hats,' he said. 'Please give me back my hats!' The hat seller got a bit cross. 'Give me my hats at once, do you hear me?'

Then he tried a different language. 'Well, maybe you don't understand English so I'll ask you in French! Donnez-moi mes chapeaux!'

But the monkeys didn't give back the hats. They carried on chattering and laughing and some people say they made so much fun of the hat seller that whatever he said, they said it back and whatever he did, they did the same.

In the end, the hat seller got completely fed up. And do you know what happened next?...............

Option 1
The hat seller took off his own hat and scratched his head. He didn't know what to do and, very crossly, he threw his hat on the ground in frustration. So the monkeys did the same. And that's how the hat seller got his hats back.

Option 2
The hat seller suddenly thought of a clever plan. He took off his own hat and threw it on the ground. And what do you think the monkeys did? They did the same. They threw their hats on the ground. And that's how the hat seller got his hats back.

The ending

Then the hat seller gathered up his hats as quick as he could and went out of the forest on his way to the town. And when he got there, didn't he have a good story to tell the people who came to buy his hats?

Bringing the story to life

The story gives lots of opportunities for actions and sounds. For instance, when the hat seller is trying to get his hats back, you can:

▶ make monkey sounds and monkey gestures – the children can join in with these

▶ vary your voice to sound pleading, cross, commanding, frustrated.

Follow-up activities

▶ Hats...hats...hats – make them, bring them, paint them, use them for role-play.

Pinonçita

This story comes from Chile. The traditional version is about a little boy, Pinonçito, who is born after his mother has been given a piñon fruit to bring her luck. Here the main character has been changed to be a little girl and the story starts after her birth. The story may remind you of various others – Tom Thumb, Thumbelina, Roald Dahl's 'James and the Giant Peach' and the Mrs Pepperpot stories.

Pronunciation

For Pinonçita, say Pin-yon-sita.

The basic plot

A tiny little child suffers a series of adventures:

▶ nearly getting drowned

▶ hiding under a mushroom which is put in a saucepan of stew

▶ being spooned into a mouth

▶ escaping onto a field of grass

▶ being swallowed by a donkey

▶ getting out of the donkey and picked up by a bird

▶ being placed in a birds' nest and threatened by a snake

▶ frightening the snake and earning the reward of being taken home

▶ finding a magic bone and rolling it home

and the final adventure – rolling the bone home - makes the child grow to a normal size.

Preparation

A little collection of props can represent the different stages of Pinonçita's adventures – the mushroom where she hides, the saucepan into which she is tipped, the donkey that swallows her up, the bird that flies her into the sky, the nest where the mother-bird takes her, the snake that threatens the little birds, the magic bone she has to find.

You could hide replica objects in a colourful bag or box and bring them out to introduce the story.

As the storyteller you can say:

Here's a story I have to tell you and these are some of the things you will find in the story.

The Story

Once there was a tiny little girl who never grew any bigger. The little girl's name was Pinonçita.

And her mother had to make special tiny things for her – tiny clothes, a tiny little bed, a tiny little pillow, a tiny spoon ... Pinonçita's mother was very worried about her. She was worried she might get squashed. That's why she always said, 'Don't go out when I'm not here.'

But one day, when Pinonçita's mother was out at the market, Pinonçita went out into the garden and into the field at the back of her house. Out there, everything looked enormous!

Then suddenly it started to rain. Great big drops made great big puddles and Pinonçita thought she might drown. She looked around for a place to be safe and when she saw a mushroom, it seemed to be just what she needed. It looked like an umbrella. So she climbed up the stalk and hid under the top. 'Now,' she said, 'I'm safe.'

But just then, some mushroom pickers came along and picked the mushroom where Pinonçita was hiding. Suddenly she was in a basket, then in a house in a kitchen, then in the middle of a saucepan of stew. It was very very hot!! What could Pinonçita do?

She didn't want to get eaten!

Now she saw a big big spoon that came dipping down towards her in the saucepan of stew. Suddenly she was on the spoon, still holding onto her mushroom, and now she was going into a mouth!! There were white teeth inside and a big pink tongue and Pinonçita wanted to get out. What could she do?

Suddenly Pinonçita got a good idea. She tickled the inside of the mouth – and the mouth spat her out. Pinonçita went flying through the air and landed outside the door on the grass in a farmyard. She rolled over and over to clean herself up. But then a donkey came along, saw Pinonçita and swallowed her up. It thought she was something nice to eat. Now Pinonçita was inside a donkey!! What could she do?

Pinonçita had a good idea. She tickled the inside of the donkey's tummy and the donkey coughed and spat her out. Now she landed on the grass again. Once more she rolled over to clean herself up. But unfortunately, a bird was flying past at that moment. And when the bird saw Pinonçita, she thought the little girl was a worm. So the bird flew down and picked her up in its mouth!! What could Pinonçita do?

As the bird flew into the sky, Pinonçita called out, 'Help, help!' And the mother-bird heard and said, 'What's that?' 'It's me,' said Pinonçita. 'I'm not a worm, I'm a little girl.' 'Oh dear,' the mother-bird said. 'You'd better come to my nest. I'll look after you there.'

So that's how Pinonçita ended up in a bird's nest with baby birds chirping all round her. The mother-bird said she'd fetch her some nice juicy worms to eat. What could Pinonçita do?

When the mother-bird had flown away, Pinonçita's problems got worse. Suddenly a snake was looking into the nest and Pinonçita was very afraid. She was afraid the snake would kill the baby birds in the nest. That's why she knew she had to do something to frighten the snake away. She undid a pin that was in her dress – her mother had put it there to help keep her dress up because the dress was a bit too big – and she flashed it back and forth like a sword.

The snake was frightened. It slithered away just as the mother-bird came back. The mother-bird was grateful and pleased. She said she wanted to give Pinonçita a reward and asked her what she would like.

'I'd like to go back home,' Pinonçita said and the mother-bird said she would take her. So Pinonçita climbed on the mother-bird's back and the mother-bird flew her over the fields to her house. But she didn't take her all the way to her house – not quite! She put her down in the field nearby. Then the mother-bird told Pinonçita to look in the grass for a bone and to take the bone home to her mother.

So Pinonçita looked for a bone and when she found it, it was too big to carry. She had to roll it. But a strange thing happened. Each time she rolled the bone over, Pinonçita grew bigger and the bone got smaller. So by the time Pinonçita got near her front door, she could pick up the bone and carry it home. And when she got home, her mother was very very glad to see her. Now Pinonçita was the size of an ordinary girl and she lived happily ever after.

Follow-up activities

▶ **A theme tune for Pinonçita**
Add a little tune for Pinonçita to sing whenever she is in trouble. Whistle something you know or simply sing la-la-la-la

▶ **An extra ending**
Clinch the end of this story by saying:
And sometimes when Pinonçita grew up and had children she used to tell them the very same story that I've just told you now. Or add the well-known traditional ending:
Snip, snap snout, My tale's told out!

Remembering your story

There's no way round it. To make sure you know a story well enough to be able to tell it, you have to prepare.

Thinking about your story

If you've heard the story from someone else, you will probably remember the other person's voice as they told it. You won't have to perform the task of 'lifting the story off the page'. Instead you may have to work out how to fill gaps. If you've found the story in a book, you may need to re-read it a few times, then test your memory. You don't have to remember the actual text. Apart from particularly attractive songs, rhymes or turns of phrase, the story needs to be told in the teller's own words. When you think you have a reliable sense of the basic plot, you are ready to enjoy filling it out in your mind's eye.

Visualising the story

Eyes closed, think of your favourite scene in the story. Make a mental picture of it using all your senses – what it looks like, any sounds you can hear, textures, perfumes, the emotional atmosphere. Visualising more and more of the story by this method makes you feel as if you've been there. It becomes harder and harder to forget it.

Key words

Another method for focusing your memory is to jot down the key words of a story – just for your own practice. A key word plan of The three wishes on page 57 could look like this:

> old man
> old woman
> poor
> fairy
> three wishes
> sausage?
> one wish used
> sausage on your nose!
> two wishes gone
> money? gold cover? no!

Props

Organising props for a particular story can help focus your mind on what it's all about.

Think of one key prop that will make all the difference such as a colourful mat you could throw down for 'The cat sat on the mat' on page 54. Or try sorting out a set of props to show your audience at the beginning. Getting these out of your bag or box will help remind you of the different sections of the story as you start to tell it.

Making a story map

Drawing a bird's eye view of a story can help fix in your mind the locations and shape of the story. Take a large sheet of paper and some coloured pens and plot all the places in your story on the page before you. Houses, castles, forests, animal dens – make little drawings or doodles on your map to represent the various elements. Story maps of simple journey stories can be made by your audience too, providing a highly stimulating follow-on activity.

Story cards

Supply yourself with a number of file cards. Then make up titles for each main scene in your story and jot them down, one per card. If you like, add relevant doodles or drawings.

Now you have a useful memory-aid which can also be used during your storytelling. As you progress through the story, you can lay out each card in front of you, saying (quite dramatically, if you wish), 'Now let's see what happened next.'

Managing storytime

It's not just the stories which make a satisfying Storytime. Other practical issues make a difference too.

When

A usual routine is for storytelling sessions to occur at the end of a morning or afternoon. The pattern has its plus-points such as calming children down before going home. But there are several disadvantages, from mothers and carers waiting at the door to tiredness on the part of children and staff. A good idea is to consider bringing Storytime forward, not necessarily every day of the week but sufficiently regularly to enable children to be bright and active in taking part. An earlier time also gives opportunity for follow-on activities.

Where

Finding or creating a good space for Storytime is not always easy. A small cosy room can be helpful but most people have to use the space they've got. If there is an alternative to your book corner, this is usually a preferable area unless you are happy about children reaching out for books for you to read on demand. You can create a focal point by draping a few brightly coloured cloths behind you.

Seating

Storytelling is often associated with comfy armchairs. But many storytellers find these limiting. A low chair brings you more to the children's level and makes it easier to move your arms about. For your audience, it is far preferable to sit in a wide horseshoe two or three lines deep than eight or nine lines back in a crowded space. As well as enabling better eye contact, it is easier for you to show your props or have children come out to the front without tripping over everyone else.

Length of session

When children first come to their Early Years provision and are new to Storytime, their ability to concentrate in a group is normally very short. A few rhymes or songs and a short chant or story are enough. By the time children are 4 or 5 years old, they can enjoy 30 minutes or more if Storytime is varied, participative and fun.

Who

A vital question is how many children and what age ranges are acceptable. More than about 20–25 children is probably too many, except perhaps on a special occasion. There can be advantages in having older and younger children together if only from time to time. Support from other adults is also of great assistance, providing help in encouraging children's responses and sorting out problems. Some venues find it useful to have additional storytelling sessions for particular small groups, for instance of children who don't usually speak.

Difficult situations

Storytelling gives opportunity to manage behaviour through the storytelling itself rather than through such disciplinary methods as asking children to sit up and be quiet. Repetition of rhythms, rhymes and actions can regain the attention of those who are getting fidgety or distracted. There need to be agreed strategies about dealing with difficult behaviour, but again it is best to try and win attention through the stories. Interruptions from other adults can also be problematic and need to be minimised: the message should be that storytelling deserves undivided attention.

The wider context

Although storytelling is highly sociable, storytellers can sometimes feel isolated. It helps to consider the wider context.

Involve your colleagues

Talking with colleagues is one of the best ways to get over the worry about other adults witnessing your storytelling. You could usefully discuss questions such as what should go on in Storytime and how to manage difficult behaviour on the part of some children.

You might then feel better about trying to involve as many adults as possible in Storytime itself. Colleagues can either give support by helping with the children or by sharing the storytelling itself.

Involve parents

Parents often do not realise just how valuable it is to talk and tell stories with their children. Some may underestimate the value of the activity because they think that education is really about learning to read and write. You could give parents handouts of some of the rhymes or stories you are working on. They may appreciate knowing the words! Or maybe they could be invited to join a special Storytime or attend a short talk about storytelling.

Get involved with people in the rest of your setting or school

Although storytelling for young children is just as important as for the older ones, Early Years groups often get neglected when there is a school Book Week or Arts Week. It is vital for the younger children to be included. Wider links can also be formed through such projects as when older children in a school create stories for the younger ones and visit to tell them their stories.

Arrange for some storytelling training

People working with children are generally expected to be able to tell stories as if by magic. All too often they have received little training or advice on how to go about it. A real confidence booster can be provided by some straightforward storytelling training. There are plenty of professional storytellers who should be able to help with an INSET session. Equally useful is for staff to get together on their own account to share stories, ideas and techniques.

Invite a professional storyteller to visit

A professional storyteller can support and complement your regular storytelling work by raising the status of storytelling, supplying you with new stories and offering fresh approaches to the storytelling itself. One way to help fund a visit is by grouping together with other venues. Or try persuading your local Early Years development team to improve the profile of storytelling in your area by arranging storytelling sessions for the children and training for the staff.

Join a storytelling club

Storytelling clubs for adults now exist in many places across the country and are evidence of the widespread renewal of interest in storytelling that has taken place in recent years. They are one way of getting into the swing. Another is to attend the growing number of storytelling performances at festivals, arts centres and libraries. You can find out about such events from the Society for Storytelling, the Internet or local arts newsletters.

Stories, Books and Resources

One of the abiding tasks for all storytellers is seeking out fresh stories, new approaches to storytelling and like-minded people.

Finding stories by word of mouth

▶ Look into your own memory and you might discover all kinds of half-forgotten things from your own childhood as well as anecdotes of your own experience and tales you just about remember and could probably tell with a bit of preparation.

▶ Ask friends and relatives for stories they remember and you might be surprised at what they have got up their sleeve. A good way to prompt their recollection is by recounting a story of your own.

▶ Share with colleagues and you could help create a new core collection of oral stories at your place of work. This is a good way to increase everyone's repertoire.

▶ Listen to professional storytellers and you might pick up another good children's story to add to your core collection. This is how folktales and myths were kept alive before they got written down.

Finding stories from published material

▶ Stories on tape and CD offer a comparatively easy way to increase your knowledge of stories. A catalogue of tapes and CDs recorded by professional storytellers is available from the Society for Storytelling (see p75).

▶ Individual picture books offer the chance to find strong, simple retellings of a wide variety of folktales, myths and legends from different cultures around the world.

▶ Collections of traditional stories offer a wide range of material to choose from. Some are written specifically with younger children in mind. But you might have to read quite a lot of stories before finding one you really like. Some collections to try include:

Hugh Lupton, The Story Tree – Tales to Read Aloud
(Barefoot Books)

Sophie Windham, The Orchard Book of Nursery Stories
(Orchard Books)

Mary Medlicott (ed), The King with Dirty Feet and The Big-Wide-Mouthed Toad-Frog
(Kingfisher Books)

▶ The Internet can connect you to many sites containing collections of folktales and other stories.

Finding out more about storytelling

▶ Some of the classic texts about storytelling with children are no longer in print but are available from libraries. These include:

Eileen Colwell, Storytelling
(Thimble Press, 1991).

Betty Rosen, Shapers and Polishers
(Mary Glasgow Publications, 1991).

▶ Guides to storytelling in schools include:

Teresa Grainger, Traditional Storytelling in the Primary Classroom
(Scholastic, 1997).

Elizabeth Grugeon and Paul Gardner, The Art of Storytelling for Teachers and Pupils
(David Fulton, 2000).

► Various organisations can provide details of storytelling clubs and festivals and forthcoming events, directories of storytellers and information packs:

The Society for Storytelling, P.O. Box 2344,
Reading RG6 7FG. Tel: 0118 935 1381.

The Scottish Storytelling Centre, 43-45 High Street,
Edinburgh EH1 1SR. Tel: 0131 556 9579.

The Verbal Arts Centre, Stable Lane and Mill Wall, Bishop Street, Derry,
Northern Ireland BT48 6PU. Tel: 028 7126 6946.

Continuity and progression

The **Baby & Beyond™** series takes simple activities or resources and shows how they can be used with children at each of the EYFS development stages, from birth to 60+ months. Each double page spread covers one activity, so you can see the progression at a glance.

Shows how simple resources can be used by children at different ages and stages

Inspiration for planning continuous provision

Messy Play	978-1-905019-58-8
The Natural World	978-1-905019-57-1
The Sensory World	978-1-905019-60-1
Sound and Music	978-1-905019-59-5
Mark Making	978-1-905019-78-6
Construction	978-1-905019-77-9
Dolls & Soft Toys	978-1-905019-80-9
Bikes, Prams, Pushchairs	978-1-905019-76-2
Role Play	978-1-906029-02-9
Finger Play & Rhymes	978-1-906029-01-2
Dens & Shelters	978-1-906029-03-6
Food	978-1-906029-04-3

To see the full range of Featherstone books visit www.acblack.com

through the EYFS

Ideal to support progression and extend learning.

If you have found this book useful you might also like ...

LB Making Poetry
ISBN 978-1-4081-1250-2

LB Christmas
ISBN 978-1-9022-3364-2

LB Discovery Bottles
ISBN 978-1-9060-2971-5

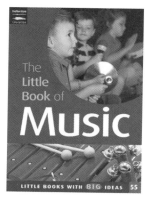

LB Music
ISBN 978-1-9041-8754-7

All available from
www.acblack.com/featherstone

The Little Books Club

There is always something in Little Books to help and inspire you.
Packed full of lovely ideas, Little Books meet the need for exciting and
practical activities that are fun to do, address the Early Learning Goals
and can be followed in most settings. Everyone is a winner!

We publish 5 new Little Books a year. Little Books Club members receive
each of these 5 books as soon as they are published for a reduced price.
The subscription cost is £37.50 – a one off payment that buys
the 5 new books for £7.50 instead of £8.99 each.

In addition to this, Little Books Club Members receive:
· Free postage and packing on anything ordered from the
  Featherstone catalogue
· A 15% discount voucher upon joining which can be used to buy any
  number of books from the Featherstone catalogue
· Members price of £7.50 on any additional Little Book purchased
· A regular, free newsletter dealing with club news, special offers and
  aspects of Early Years curriculum and practice
· All new Little Books on approval - return in good condition within 30
  days and we'll refund the cost to your club account

Call 020 7440 2446 or email: littlebooks@acblack.com for
an enrolment pack. Or download an application form from our website:

www.acblack.com/featherstone

The **Little Books** series consists of:

All Through the Year

Bags, Boxes & Trays

Bricks and Boxes

Celebrations

Christmas

Circle Time

Clay and Malleable
Materials

Clothes and Fabrics

Colour, Shape and Number

Cooking from Stories

Cooking Together

Counting

Dance

Dance, with music CD

Discovery Bottles

Dough

50

Fine Motor Skills

Fun on a Shoestring

Games with Sounds

Growing Things

ICT

Investigations

Junk Music

Language Fun

Light and Shadow

Listening

Living Things

Look and Listen

Making Books and Cards

Making Poetry

Mark Making

Maths Activities

Maths from Stories

Maths Songs and Games

Messy Play

Music

Nursery Rhymes

Outdoor Play

Outside in All Weathers

Parachute Play

Persona Dolls

Phonics

Playground Games

Prop Boxes for Role Play

Props for Writing

Puppet Making

Puppets in Stories

Resistant Materials

Role Play

Sand and Water

Science through Art

Scissor Skills

Sewing and Weaving

Small World Play

Sound Ideas

Storyboards

Storytelling

Seasons

Time and Money

Time and Place

Treasure Baskets

Treasureboxes

Tuff Spot Activities

Washing Lines

Writing

All available from

www.acblack.com/featherstone